THE PYRAMID OF SELF

Brian Dehler

The Pyramid of Self
Written by Brian Dehler

Published by Master Key Society
Saint Paul, Minnesota

The author and publisher have made every effort to ensure the
accuracy and completeness of the information contained herein.
However, they assume no responsibility for errors, omissions, or
the outcomes of any actions taken based on this material.

This book is intended as a guide for personal development
and reflection. It is not a substitute for professional
psychological, medical, or spiritual counsel.

Library of Congress Control Number: 2025916559

ISBN: 979-8-9992806-1-9

TABLE OF CONTENTS

Preface: Read This First

Throughout history, mystery schools have safeguarded sacred knowledge—not through textbooks, but through symbols, story, and inner initiation. Their teachings were not meant to be committed to memory alone, but lived.

This book continues that tradition. Whether you are just beginning your inner work or returning after years of seeking, it meets you where you are. You don't need to understand sacred geometry, mysticism, or philosophy in advance. What matters is your openness to listen and reflect.

Several of America's Founding Fathers studied within esoteric traditions. They embedded their insights into the Great Seal of the United States, adopted in 1782. At the time, seals were created in wax and designed to be viewed on both sides. Following this tradition, the United States Seal bears two images: on the obverse, the bald eagle clutching arrows and an olive branch; on the reverse, the unfinished pyramid crowned with the Eye of Providence (or All-Seeing Eye). Today, both appear on every U.S. dollar bill, carrying a message few truly notice. For this book, we turn our attention to the pyramid.

The pyramid is not merely a relic of ancient wisdom; it is a living framework, a blueprint for conscious evolution, and a call to action. You are not merely here to learn. You are here to reclaim your role as a conscious creator of your reality.

The canonical text that follows was written as a companion meditation on the reverse of the Seal. It stands as the cornerstone of this book. Let it speak to your intuition. Return to it often. Let your curiosity guide you. The chapters ahead will help illuminate its deeper meanings.

The Pyramid of Self

Within you is the Master Key
to all creation.

What is above is reflected below,
what is within is mirrored without.
May the one great work be completed.

The journey begins in unity.
Spirit descending into form.
The spiritual self on high
to the material self on low.

From this connection, the spark of the divine.
The process of becoming whole.
The fragmented aspects of your being
harmonize under the light of divine awareness.
Out of many, one.

When you align the Lower Self with the Higher Self,
the creator awakens.

The energy of creative chaos appears.
Waves of potentiality are in a state of confusion.
Through intention, balance, and action,
the chaos transmutes into harmony, purpose, and order.

Manifest the Higher Self through creative action.
Allow the essence of the divine
to take tangible form in the material world.

The elements guide the way:
Earth grounds and builds.
Water cleanses and nurtures.
Air brings clarity and insight.
Fire ignites passion and transformation.
The Spirit unites.

In equilibrium lies mastery.

The pyramid is your map.
A framework of creation.
Its base provides the stability,
while its apex shines with the light of the All-Seeing Eye,
the divine awareness that connects you to eternal source.

Take responsibility for your path.
Become both the builder and the creation.

With time, each choice and each moment
becomes another stone upon your foundation.
The spiral of life winds upward.
Layers of experience reflect growth,
the concentric phases of your journey.

Intuition is the voice of the Higher Self.
Follow your guide and trust in its hand,
even when the way seems rocky.
The journey is the reward.
Every step brings wisdom.
Every step brings clarity.

Aimlessness is the shadow of the self unclaimed.
It is fear made manifest.
If you do not direct your journey, another will.
It is better to choose, to err, and to refine.
Do not remain lost in indecision.
Take your step.

When your pyramid nears completion,
it reveals not an ending, but the eternal truth:
you are both the beginning and the end,
the question and the answer,
the journey and the destination.

You are the creator and the creation.
This is the new order for the ages.

Align with your true self,
and the universe will unfold in your favor

THE REVERSE OF THE GREAT
SEAL OF THE UNITED STATES

Chapter 1: An Invitation to the Journey

Every so often, a symbol appears that seems to veil deeper meaning. This book explores one such symbol, visible daily yet rarely truly seen: the pyramid on the Great Seal of the United States, printed on every U.S. dollar bill.

Within this emblem lies a powerful blueprint for personal growth, revealing a threefold journey:

1. Self-Realization
2. Divine Manifestation
3. Discovery of your Master Key

As you read, you'll encounter universal principles drawn from ancient mystery schools, esoteric traditions, and natural laws that echo the cosmos itself. At the heart of these teachings is the idea that transformation begins from within, and that your life can reflect higher wisdom once aligned with intention.

The essence of this journey lies in integration. Stay attuned to the ideas that stir something within you: a flash of curiosity, a moment of insight. That spark is your inner compass guiding you toward deeper awareness. If a phrase or image lingers, let it. Its meaning may unfold over time.

This is more than a book of theories; it is a guide to an inward journey, inviting personal revelation and lasting transformation.

Symbols carry power, and those chosen to represent a nation often hold significance far beyond their original intent. Notice the pyramid's unfinished apex, a purposeful gap that signifies potential. It is both an ideal and a calling. Above it, the All-Seeing Eye invites you to transcend the material realm and perceive greater truths about existence.

So why was this symbol chosen to represent a new nation?

Because reality is shaped by three essential forces: clarity of desire, unwavering belief, and deliberate action. Simple in essence, though not always easy, these forces carry immense power, reflecting deep self-awareness, focused intention, and inner alignment.

When recognized, the pyramid becomes more than a symbol. It becomes a sigil.

Our hope is that by the time you complete this book, a seed will have been planted. One that grows into a life aligned with your most authentic self. And as you move into that alignment, your world will begin to shift, often in unexpected and extraordinary ways.

Chapter 2: The Seal and Its Esoteric History

In 1776, as America's Founding Fathers sought a national emblem, they turned to ancient symbolism to express the endurance and ideals of their revolutionary vision. After several revisions, the final design was adopted in 1782: an unfinished pyramid rising toward an illuminated Eye of Providence.

The pyramid's thirteen layers represent the original colonies and reflect strength through unity. The capstone, set apart and glowing, symbolizes divine guidance: something beyond human authority, yet intimately connected to it.

Above the pyramid, the Latin phrase *Annuit Coeptis* declares, "Our endeavor is favored." Below, *Novus Ordo Seclorum* heralds "a new order of the ages." Though intended to reflect national optimism, these phrases also carry universal meaning, pointing to spiritual guidance and the potential for personal transformation.

Symbols endure because they speak across generations. While often seen as patriotic design, the Great Seal's pyramid reflects an initiatory path: a journey of rising awareness.

The first part of the journey is Self-Realization, awakening to your higher nature and your connection to the greater whole. The second is Divine Manifestation, translating inner wisdom into action, bringing Spirit into form. The third is The Master Key, fully integrating higher awareness with practical living.

Whether the designers consciously intended these deeper meanings or were guided by something unseen, the result is undeniable: the Great Seal encodes a spiritual journey echoed across cultures.

Even in modern history, the symbol retained its esoteric roots. During the Great Depression, President Franklin D. Roosevelt, himself a 33rd degree Scottish Rite Freemason, was influenced by then-Secretary of Agriculture, Henry A. Wallace, a fellow Freemason and student of Theosophy, Hermeticism, and Rosicrucian philosophy. Their shared understanding of these traditions inspired the decision to place the Great Seal on the back of the one-dollar bill in 1935.

To them, it wasn't just a national emblem. It was a spiritual reminder: each person is building their own inner pyramid, one choice at a time.

Seen this way, the pyramid is neither decorative nor abstract. It's a subtle call to higher consciousness. An invitation to build your life with purpose.

In the next chapter, we'll move beyond symbols to explore the cosmic rhythms that shape your path and reveal the deeper geometry of your own evolution.

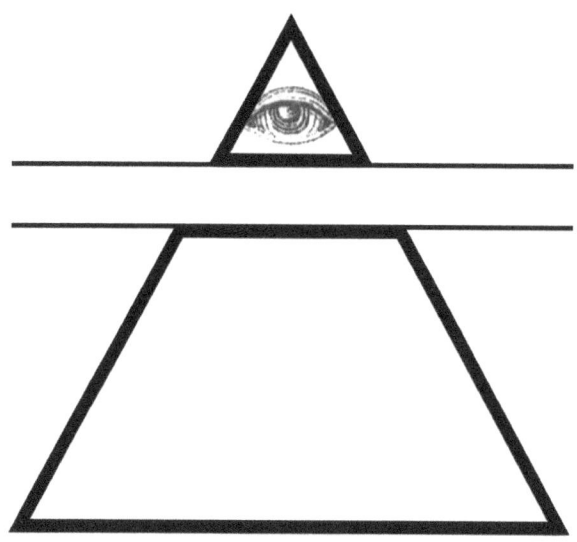

Chapter 3: The Celestial Dance
Venus and the Rose

Long before humanity carved symbols into stone or raised temples to the sky, our ancestors looked upward for guidance. The night sky became their first sacred text, and among its most luminous teachers was Venus, the brightest celestial wanderer.

For thousands of years, careful observations noted Venus's graceful rhythm. Over an eight-year cycle, the planet traces a five-pointed star, a near-perfect pentagram, in the sky. This isn't a coincidence. It's a pattern of extraordinary elegance, revealing a deeper order woven into the fabric of creation.

As Venus orbits the Sun, it completes five synodic cycles, each lasting 584 days. Each time, it returns to nearly the same point in the sky, forming the points of this celestial rose. Ancient civilizations didn't view this pattern as just an astronomical curiosity. They saw it as evidence of divine intelligence: an invitation to align with the deeper rhythms of the cosmos.

Creation, they believed, unfolds in accordance with sacred timing. Aligning yourself with that rhythm invites harmony, clarity, and profound inner alignment.

The Rose of Venus became a symbol of spiritual refinement. It reflected not only the structure of the heavens, but also the architecture of transformation within us. Just as the pyramid charts your ascent from the physical to the divine, the Rose mirrors the cyclical nature of inner growth, not as a straight line, but as a spiral of evolution and return.

As we continue, you'll begin to see how this celestial Rose relates to the five elemental forces within you. These same patterns, etched in the stars, live in your thoughts, your choices, and your becoming.

Chapter 4: Sacred Geometry in Nature

Nature expresses its intelligence through patterns: spirals, ratios, and repetitions that echo across all forms of life. From galaxies to seashells, tree branches to flower petals, there is an underlying order. This order is known as sacred geometry, a bridge between the physical and the divine.

Across history, humans have recognized these recurring patterns as blueprints of creation. Ancient architects embedded sacred geometry into pyramids, temples, and cathedrals, not for decoration, but to align physical space with spiritual principle. These patterns weren't just seen as beautiful; they were purposeful.

Civilizations from Egypt and Greece to India and Mesoamerica wove sacred proportions into their most revered monuments. They believed that certain shapes, angles, and ratios could connect humanity to universal harmony and raise consciousness.

Among the most profound of these patterns is the Golden Ratio: Phi, approximately 1.618. Found in seashells, pinecones, rotation of hurricanes, and even proportions of the human body, this ratio appears throughout the natural world. When used in art or design, it resonates deeply with human perception, evoking a sense of balance and beauty.

The Fibonacci Sequence is another. Each number is the sum of the two before it: 1, 1, 2, 3, 5, 8, 13... This simple progression appears in leaf arrangements, flower petals, branching trees, and DNA. It's a rhythm of expansion seen throughout nature, suggesting a living intelligence guiding growth from the smallest forms of life to the cosmos itself.

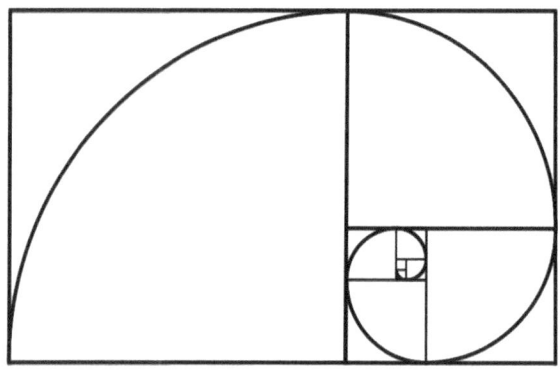

Sacred geometry isn't just theoretical. When you begin to see these patterns around and within you, life feels less random and more resonant. Recognizing this order invites deeper clarity, balance, and trust in the intelligence behind creation.

And yet, we perceive only a sliver of what's truly there. Human vision registers less than 0.0035% of the electromagnetic spectrum. Our other senses are just as limited. Reality extends far beyond what we can physically sense.

Still, we intuit more than we see. For example, scopaesthesia is that subtle sense of being watched, or magnetoreception, an ability found in some animals and possibly humans, to sense the Earth's magnetic field for orientation and navigation, hints at the body's deeper intelligence. Ancient cultures didn't dismiss these sensations; they understood them as windows into a hidden dimension of truth.

In the next chapter, we'll explore how sacred geometry is not only written into the world around you, but it lives within you. Through the five elements—Earth, Water, Air, Fire, and Spirit—you'll begin to see your own being as a reflection of the same intelligence that guides the stars.

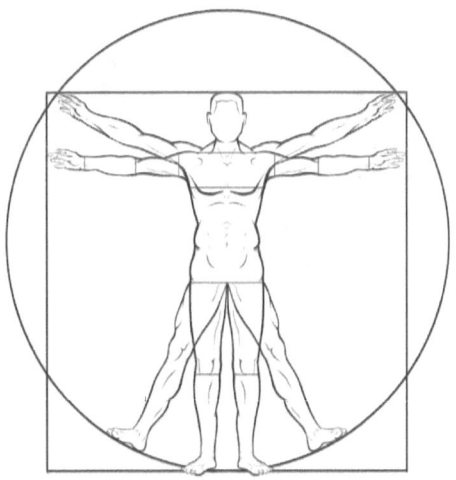

"Learn how to see. Realize that everything connects to everything else." – Leonardo da Vinci

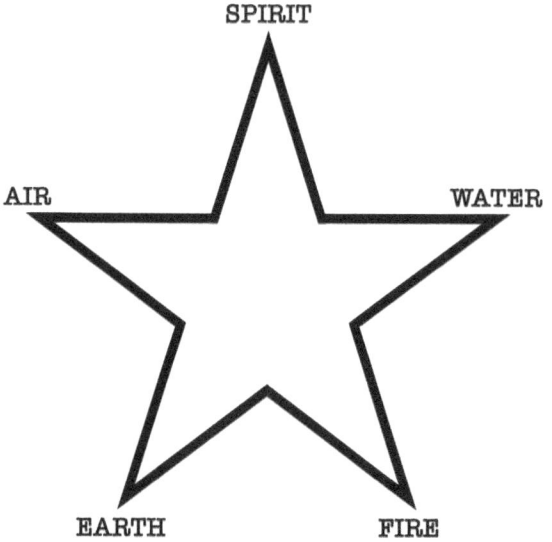

Chapter 5: The Rose Within
The Five Elements of Self

To our ancestors, the sky was not just a source of light and weather; it was a symbolic framework, a map of divine truth. The Rose, the five-pointed star traced by Venus, was more than just a beautiful sight. It was meaningful. It symbolized the interplay of five essential forces within us: Earth, Water, Air, Fire, and Spirit.

Ancient traditions taught that both the cosmos and the human being are made of these elemental energies. Each one plays a vital role in the cycles of growth, healing, and transformation, not only in nature, but in your thoughts, emotions, and choices. Understanding and aligning these energies brings harmony, clarity, and wholeness.

Earth brings structure and grounding. It's the force of patience, stability, and discipline. Earth helps you build and commit.

Water governs emotion, intuition, and fluidity. It cleanses, soothes, and softens. Water helps you feel deeply and move with grace.

Air offers clarity, perspective, and communication. It helps you think clearly, speak truthfully, and perceive without distortion.

Fire fuels passion and transformation. It sparks willpower, action, and creative courage. Fire helps you move, change, and dare.

Spirit, or **Aether**, is the unifying field. It connects you to your Higher Self and to the divine source behind all forms. It is the space within which all the other elements exist.

When you consciously engage these five forces, you begin restoring inner balance. You stop reacting to life and start shaping it, intentionally and from within.

Like Venus's path through the heavens, your own growth unfolds in elegant spirals. You move between clarity and confusion, action and rest, questioning and knowing. But each turn brings you a little closer to your most authentic self.

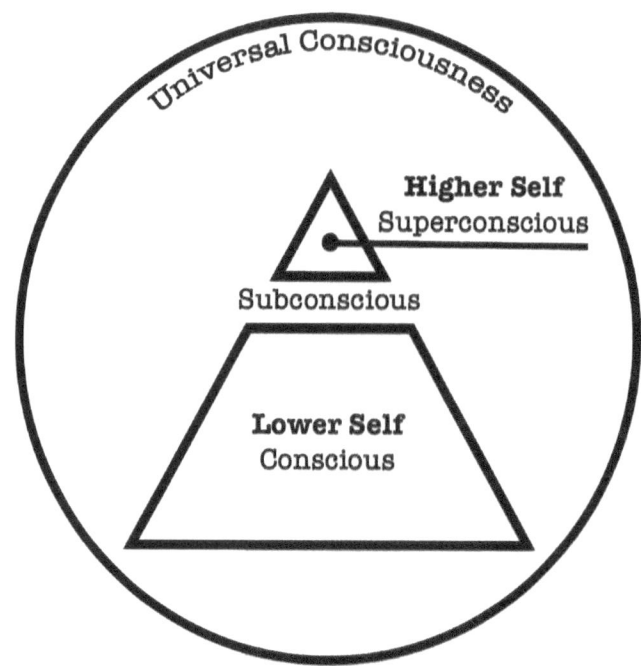

Chapter 6: The Higher Self
Your Divine Connection

At the heart of the spiritual journey is the Higher Self: a timeless creative presence within you that transcends form, space, and time. In other traditions, it may be called the superconscious, the creative self, the soul, the muse, or even your future self—the perfected version you are becoming. Whatever term you choose, this is your most expansive identity. It offers guidance from beyond the limits of ordinary perception.

Within your being are multiple layers of consciousness, each playing a distinct role in your growth and awakening. Your Lower Self is everyday awareness, tied closely to ego, identity, and survival instincts. It navigates practical life and tends to operate through habit and reaction.

Next is the Subconscious, a deeper layer that links body and mind. It stores memories, beliefs, and emotions, often influencing you beneath conscious awareness. Represented as the gap in the Pyramid, the Subconscious serves as a bridge—translating subtle impressions from the Higher Self into dreams, emotional cues, and gut instincts.

While the Subconscious translates, the Higher Self is the source—holding your highest wisdom and purpose. It guides you gently, not with force or volume, but with subtle knowing—those flashes of insight, intuition, or sudden clarity that feel more like remembering than discovering.

Beyond even the Higher Self is Universal Consciousness—the interconnected field of energy and intelligence that encompasses all beings and experiences.

Just as mystics speak of The All, the boundless intelligence behind all form, so too have physicists identified a unifying field beneath matter: the quantum field. In quantum physics, all particles arise as fluctuations within these invisible fields, forming what some describe as a sea of potential.

This field is not inert. In certain experiments, the act of observation appears to influence the outcome. While the nature of this phenomenon remains open to interpretation, it follows the ancient teachings: that reality is shaped, in part, by relationship and awareness.

The Higher Self as a drop from the ocean of
Universal Consciousness, descending through the
element of Spirit (Aether) to meet the Lower Self.

In this way, science and spirituality converge—not through identical language, but through shared wonder. Both point toward a truth long sensed: that consciousness and creation are intimately connected, and that reality may be far more participatory than once believed.

In the journey of the Pyramid, the Higher Self is not an isolated pinnacle, but a focusing point within that greater field of Universal Consciousness.

Unlike the Lower Self, which is grounded in physical experience and linear thought, the Higher Self perceives from a broader vantage. It sees across time, senses hidden patterns, and gently steers you toward alignment with your deeper potential.

When your Lower Self aligns with the Higher Self, something profound happens. Life begins to flow. Decisions feel natural. Synchronicities appear. You are no longer forcing outcomes—you are responding from a place of inner clarity. This state is often described as being "in flow."

Modern science now recognizes the digestive tract as a "second brain" (the enteric nervous system)—containing a neural network that influences emotion, perception, and decision-making. That intuitive "gut feeling"? It is both biological and spiritual. It is your body, translating the subtle language of the Higher Self.

This relationship is alive. It is not fixed or static, but responsive—like breath, or flame. When the Lower Self resists, the connection dims. But when you listen, soften, and act in alignment, the bridge strengthens. Every moment offers an opportunity to deepen the connection.

And here is the paradox: the Higher Self has always been with you. It is not something you must earn or become. It has always lived within you, waiting to be remembered.

The spiritual path, then, is not about becoming someone else. It is about removing what obscures who you've always been.

In the next chapter, we'll step into the first stage of your conscious journey: Self-Realization, and the elemental path that guides you inward toward that remembered self.

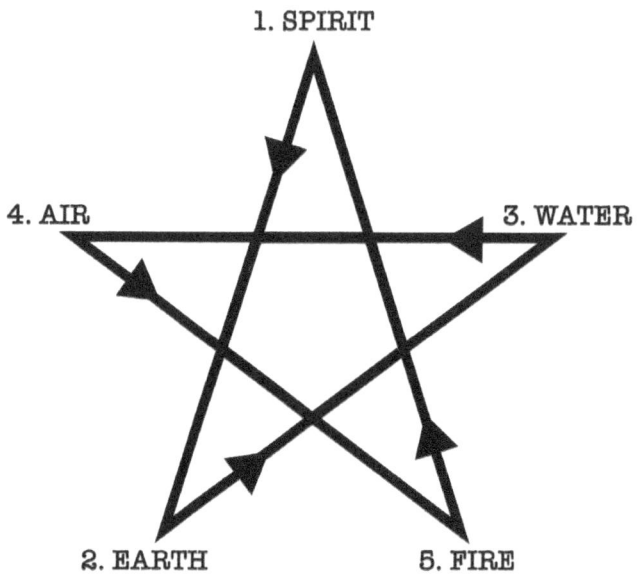

*The path to Self-Realization
by tracing the five elements in sequence.*

Chapter 7: Step 1. Self-Realization
The Path to Alignment

Self-Realization marks the first essential step in the threefold spiritual journey encoded within the pyramid. It's the moment you awaken to your deeper nature: the recognition that you are not just a product of your past, but a conscious participant in your unfolding. It's when clarity begins to rise from confusion, and something within says: There is more.

This stage is not simply about knowledge; it's about becoming. It begins the process of inner alignment, guiding your awareness, choices, and values toward something more authentic and enduring.

To move into Self-Realization, you follow a path inspired by nature itself, reflected in the celestial movement of Venus and the wisdom of the five elements. Each stage offers a kind of inner alchemy, guiding your awareness into form.

The journey begins with **Spirit**. Intention arises. A vision is felt. This is the moment of awakening—when your inner voice whispers, or roars, that something must shift.

Next is **Earth**. Here, you confront what grounds you: your habits, attachments, and structures. You begin to let go of bad habits and vices, rebuild, and create a new foundation.

Water follows. Emotion rises and is released. You allow yourself to feel, to process, and to subdue your impulses.

Then comes **Air**. Understanding takes form. Ideas find structure. Your thoughts clarify, and scattered impressions become wisdom.

Finally, **Fire**. Now, you act. Insight moves through your body. What was internal begins to manifest through behavior, change, and new momentum.

Each stage peels away a layer of illusion. With each step, you uncover more of your real self, not by force, but by following a rhythm as ancient as the stars. Just as Venus traces a rose through the heavens, your inner journey spirals through moments of learning and remembrance.

Self-realization is not a straight line. For some, clarity arrives suddenly. For others, it emerges in fragments, through rest, repetition, and reflection. However it appears for you is enough.

Pause now and take a moment to reflect on your personal journey toward Self-Realization. Consider journaling your answers to these questions:

What truth about yourself feels clearer now? What habits or beliefs no longer align with who you're becoming? Name one small yet meaningful action you can commit to today—something that reflects this newfound clarity. Remember, transformation isn't rushed; it emerges naturally through mindful action.

By noticing these inner movements, you begin to build your pyramid. One stone at a time. One moment at a time. This is the process of becoming whole. The path of Self-Realization strengthens as you walk it, until the foundation within you is solid, spacious, and ready for what comes next.

From here, the journey continues into your pyramid, gradually guiding us toward Part 2: Divine Manifestation, where inner alignment becomes outward expression and inner truth becomes conscious action.

Chapter 8: As Above, So Below
The Pyramid as a Framework

The pyramid on the Great Seal is more than a historical image. It is a symbolic framework, a mirror of your spiritual development made visible.

Just as Venus draws a five-pointed star across the sky, the pyramid traces your upward path on Earth. It gives form to the invisible. It makes your inner work tangible. It reflects the architecture of conscious growth.

In ancient traditions, the pyramid represented initiation and transformation. Its wide base symbolized the grounded self: your presence in the material world. Its radiant capstone represented divine awareness, insight, and purpose. And the space between them? That is where integration lives.

The gap within the pyramid symbolizes the subconscious mind, serving as a bridge between your Higher Self and Lower Self. This bridge enables intuitive insights, intentions, and conscious desires to move freely and harmoniously between the spiritual and physical dimensions of your being. To perceive reality from this place of alignment is the state of Gnosis—the Greek word for direct knowledge and awareness. More than intellectual knowing, Gnosis is the lived experience of balance.

From above, this gap aligns with the center of the pyramid's base. It is the still point where the five elements—Earth, Water, Air, Fire, and Spirit—come into harmony. It's not a fixed destination, but a felt alignment. A state of readiness.

Crossing into this inner balance requires trust. Many approach the threshold of Gnosis but pause, waiting for certainty before moving. Yet clarity emerges through deliberate action. The light appears when you step forward.

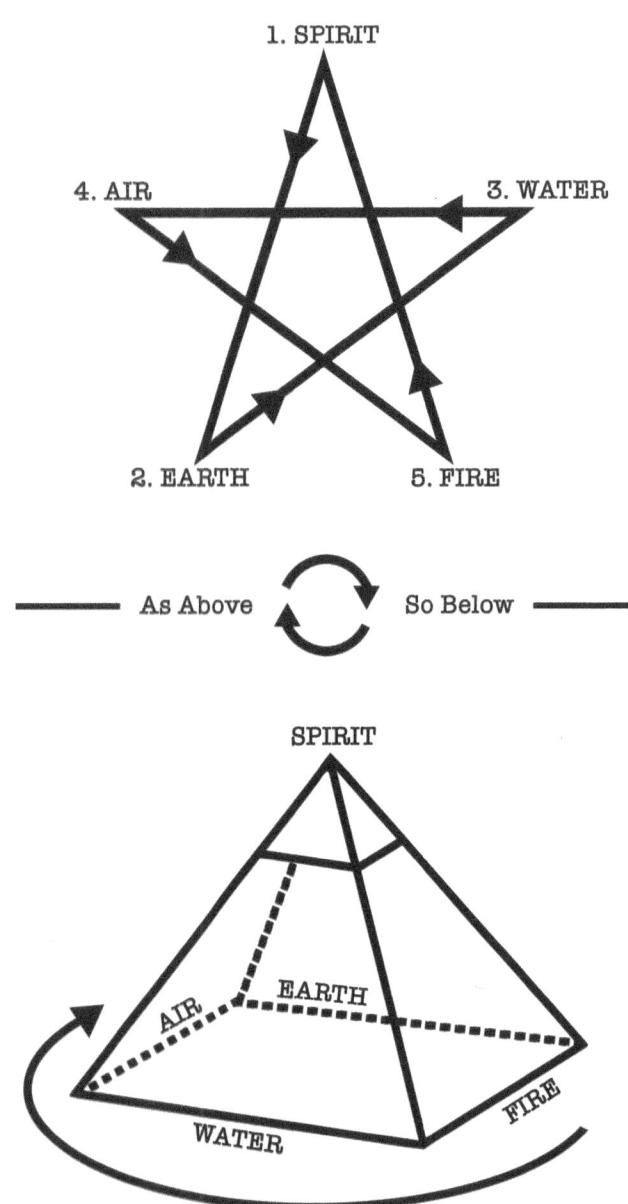

1. SPIRIT

4. AIR

3. WATER

2. EARTH

5. FIRE

As Above   So Below

SPIRIT

AIR   EARTH

WATER   FIRE

24

To enter this space is to practice subtle listening. Gnosis does not arrive as proof, but as recognition. Begin by asking fewer analytical questions and more contemplative ones: What do I already know, beneath my thinking? What feels true, even if I cannot explain it? Keep a quiet space in your day—not to escape thought, but to hear what thought obscures. Sit with symbolic images or open-ended questions. Let dreams, body sensations, and patterns in daily life become sources of guidance. Trust builds not from instant answers, but from the lived experience of seeing your intuitive impulses validated over time. Each time you move on subtle knowing, and the path opens, your confidence in Gnosis deepens.

The pyramid also teaches through movement. In Step 1, Self-Realization, you move clockwise around the base. This inward spiral represents refinement. A return to center. A drawing in of scattered energy toward stillness, clarity, and truth.

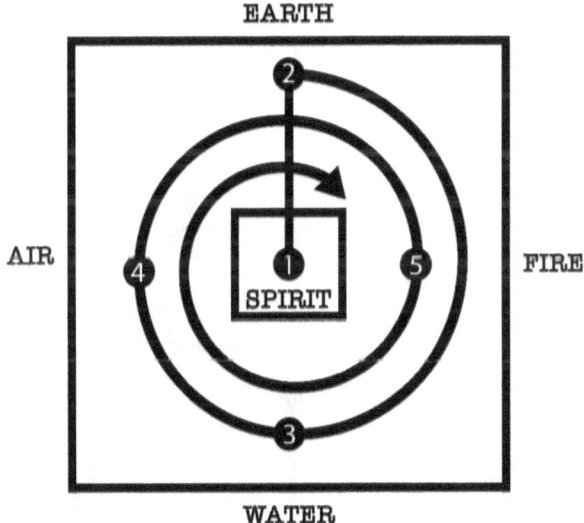

Viewing the pyramid from above.
Circumambulation around the pyramid, tracing the five elements
clockwise in an inward spiral to connect with the Higher Self.

This spiral mirrors ancient rites of passage, where initiates walked a circular path, each turn drawing them closer to spiritual union. Then the direction shifts.

In Chapter 11, you'll find that in Step 2, Divine Manifestation, the movement becomes counterclockwise. Now, energy expands. The truth found within begins to shape the outer world. Insight becomes action. Purpose becomes visible.

This reversal is not a contradiction; it is completion. First inward, then outward. First silence, then speech. First becoming, then expressing.

The spiritual path isn't about escaping the world. It's about weaving spirit into it. It's the conscious choice to bring light into form.

When you understand the pyramid not as a symbol to admire, but as a process to live, you begin to move through life differently. You walk with awareness. You build intentionally. You stop waiting for permission.

In the next chapter, we'll step into the dimension of time: exploring how your personal spiral of growth unfolds through the rhythm of your life.

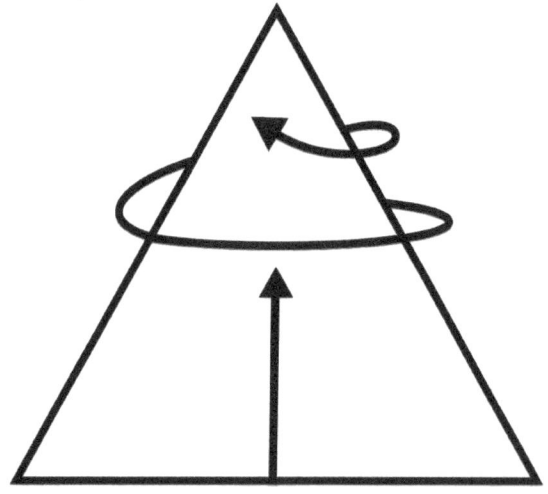

Spiraling upwards and centered.

Chapter 9: Transcending Space and Time

Having explored the pyramid as a structure of form and movement, we now step into the symbolism of time.

The Rose of Venus reflects a sacred, two-dimensional rhythm, traced in the heavens over eight-year cycles. The pyramid adds a third dimension, anchoring that rhythm into a form. But it is in the fourth dimension—time—that your personal evolution truly unfolds.

Through this lens, the pyramid becomes more than a spiritual framework. It becomes your timeline.

Each stone represents a moment. A choice. A lesson. Layer by layer, your life takes shape, built through experience, awareness, and intention.

Yet this growth is not linear. It spirals.

You revisit familiar lessons, relationships, or challenges, but each time from a new vantage point. Like climbing a spiral staircase, you return to similar terrain with greater perspective. This upward motion reflects how life refines you through repetition, rhythm, and return.

Around this spiral are concentric circles that represent phases of your life, often unfolding in cycles of roughly seven years. These phases bring changes in identity, purpose, and relationships. They shape your development not by destination, but by expansion.

The threefold journey through Self-Realization, Divine Manifestation, and The Master Key is not a single arc. It repeats. Each phase of life brings new circumstances that ask you to revisit these steps with deeper awareness. What once served as your foundation may become your refinement in the next cycle. You don't move backward—you spiral upward.

This is how the steps evolve with you: familiar, yet transformed by the vantage point from which you now walk them.

Pause here and reflect: What recurring patterns or lessons have shaped you? Are there themes that seem to return with new meaning each time? Where do you feel forward motion? Where do you feel caught in repetition?

These patterns are not signs that you're stuck. They are invitations to deepen your awareness. Each return offers new perspective. Each cycle invites new choices.

You are not behind. You are not late. You are not lost.

You are in process. And that process is sacred.

Your past does not define you; it prepares you. The spiral reminds you that every step, even those that seem like detours, is part of your upward path.

Reflect on recent experiences in your life that felt difficult or challenging. Rather than seeing them as setbacks, identify the hidden lessons or gifts within these moments. Ask yourself: How did this experience strengthen or refine me? What insights can I carry forward to better navigate future challenges? In recognizing duality as your ally, you shape your path with increased confidence and clarity.

In the present moment, you lay the next stone. You do not need to know the entire plan to keep building. In the next chapter, we return to the base of the pyramid—to the checkered floor—where duality lives, and where your mastery begins.

Chapter 10: The Checkered Floor

The Dance of Duality

At the base of the pyramid lies a checkered floor, alternating squares of light and dark. This ancient symbol represents the dual nature of human experience: joy and sorrow, clarity and confusion, flow and resistance.

It reminds us that growth does not come from light alone. Wisdom emerges through contrast.

Each square is a choice. Some move you forward. Others pause your momentum. Occasionally, one may seem to lead you backward. But the goal isn't perfection. It's movement. It's awareness.

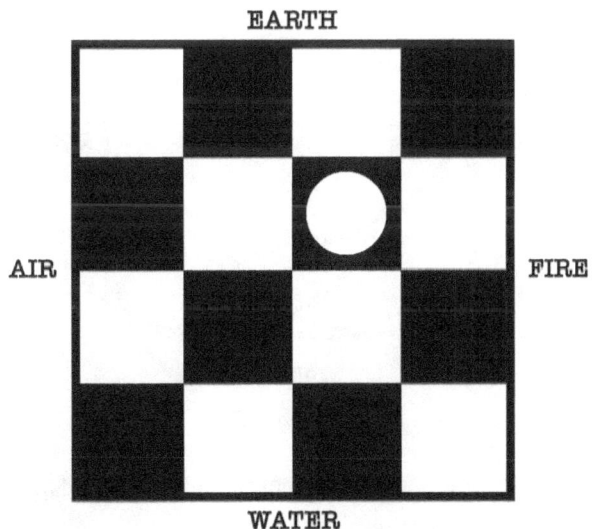

EARTH

AIR

FIRE

WATER

This checkered floor is not a static design; it is a dynamic field. The elements overlay and overlap in varying proportions in an interplay of opposites that shifts constantly. What once felt like failure can become your greatest teacher. What seemed certain may unravel, offering you the gift of humility or change. Even comfort, when unexamined, can lead to stagnation.

You've been walking this floor your entire life, since birth when you arrived on one unique square. You might say that this square is like the horoscope of your life—the guidepost that sets you on your life path. Some steps you took with full presence. Others were shaped by habits, fear, or unconscious patterns. But with each return to awareness, you reclaim authorship of your path.

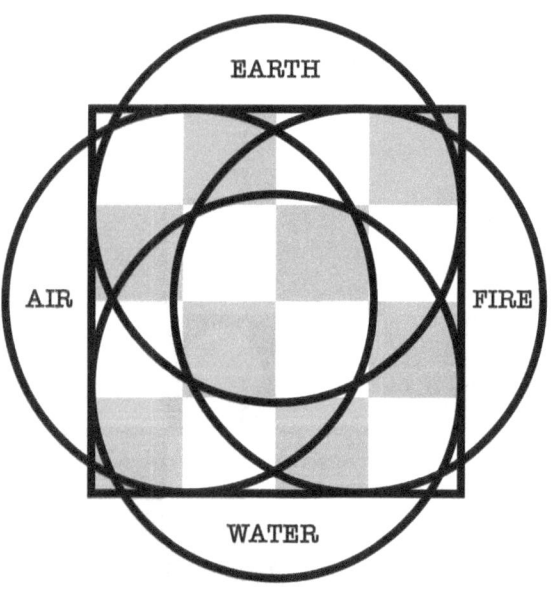

The elements upon the checkered floor overlap
and interplay in dynamic ways.

Pause and reflect: What patterns have repeated in your life? Are your steps guided by intention or reaction? Are you allowing challenge to shape you or shrink you?

Mastery is not about avoiding the dark squares. It's about navigating both light and shadow with grace, recognizing contrast as necessary—not just to growth, but to meaning.

Reflect on recent experiences in your life that felt difficult or challenging. Rather than seeing them as setbacks, identify the hidden lessons or gifts within these moments.

Ask yourself: How did this experience strengthen or refine me? What insights can I carry forward to better navigate future challenges? In recognizing duality as your ally, you reclaim your power to consciously shape your path.

The deeper truth is that duality doesn't exist to divide you; it exists to refine you. It sharpens your awareness. It stretches your capacity. And in doing so, it prepares you to live in greater alignment.

The checkered floor reminds you: no step is wasted. Every moment, regardless of how it feels, adds depth, strength, and wisdom to your foundation.

True mastery is not found in control. It's found in conscious response. In presence. In movement through contrast. In meeting life as it changes, and choosing to learn, rather than resist.

As you become more fluent in this dance, duality softens. You move closer to the center and begin to perceive the harmony woven through it all.

And from that space, you are ready to rise. The path now leads into Divine Manifestation: the outward expression of everything you've come to know.

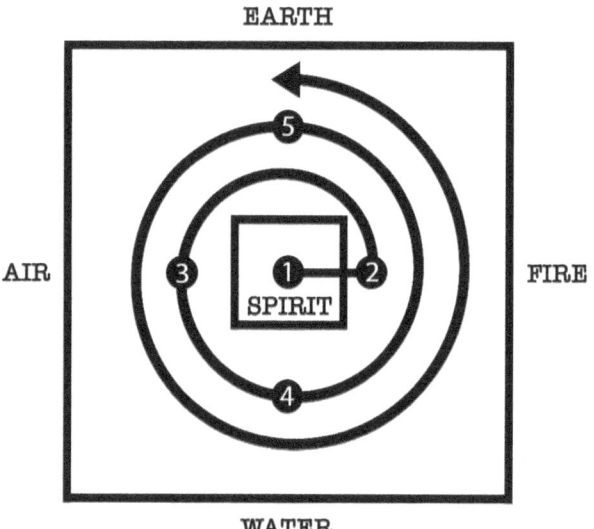

Circumambulation around the pyramid,
tracing the five elements counterclockwise in
an outward spiral to express the Higher Self.

Chapter 11: Step 2. Divine Manifestation

Bringing Spirit into Form

Divine Manifestation is Step 2 of your threefold journey. Where Step 1, Self-Realization, brought you inward, aligning you with your inner truth, this stage turns that awareness outward. Now, the task is to bring spirit into form.

This shift is reflected in the movement around the pyramid. In Step 1, Self-Realization, you circled inward, clockwise, toward clarity and balance. Now, you move outward, counterclockwise, extending your alignment into action. This is the descent of divine awareness into the physical world.

The insights you've gained are ready to be expressed. The purpose you've sensed wants to take shape.

Moving outward, the journey begins again with **Spirit**. A vision arrives. A possibility stirs. You feel the call of something that has not yet been realized.

Then comes **Fire**. Passion ignites. Energy builds. You feel the urge to move, to act, to initiate something new.

Air follows. Thought brings structure. Ideas crystallize. You begin to form a clear vision, one that can guide your steps.

Next is **Water**. Emotion checks in. You ensure that your outer direction resonates with your inner truth. You refine, soften, and align.

Finally, **Earth** grounds the process. You commit. You take steady, tangible steps. What once lived as inspiration becomes something others can see, feel, and touch.

This sequence doesn't require perfection; it asks for presence. Many people linger too long in vision without acting. Others act prematurely, without clarity. True manifestation arises when all the elements work in harmony.

Identify one clear vision or inspired idea you've been holding but not yet acted upon fully. Write down one simple, tangible action you can take within the next 24 hours to begin bringing this vision to life. Consider this your commitment to yourself— to your divine potential made manifest through aligned action.

Divine Manifestation is a dance. You don't need to control every outcome. You need only to listen, to trust what you've already come to know, and to move with courage and care.

This phase is not about ambition. It's about authenticity. It's about allowing the truth within you to take form through consistent, aligned action.

Learn to listen to your "gut feeling." Open yourself up to the call to adventure. The calling within that speaks through your curiosity and instinctual feelings.

In the first step of self-realization, you focused on overcoming the ego through self-refinement and looking inward. Now you are called to focus on your Higher Self. The authentic you that yearns to express itself.

And as you embody what you've realized, you begin to shift not only your own life but the lives of others around you.

What was once silent becomes visible. What was once potential becomes purpose. What was once unseen becomes creation.

And all of it prepares you for what comes next: The Master Key. The moment when the inner and outer meet, fully and finally, revealing the state of integration.

Chapter 12: Step 3. The Master Key
Equilibrium of Self

The Master Key represents the final phase of your three-step journey. It is the full integration of your Higher and Lower Self, where inner wisdom and outer action move as one. Intuition flows into behavior. Insight becomes embodiment.

You now possess the power to manifest your future as the co-creator of your reality. In Step 1, Self-Realization, you aligned yourself with your Higher Self and developed faith in yourself. In Step 2, Divine Manifestation, you learned to listen to your authentic Higher Self and to allow its expression to move through you by acting on intuition. Now, in Step 3, you consciously direct your desires.

To do this, begin by identifying what it is you truly want. Be honest and precise. Go beyond vague longing—and beyond what you think you're supposed to want. Let go of what feels acceptable, impressive, or safe. Speak from the heart. Clarify the specific form your desire wants to take. Then, go deeper—ask yourself why. Why does this matter to you? Why now? You may have many goals throughout your life—or even many at once. But it is through the clear pursuit of even one that inner alignment begins to take form. And the more concentrated and singular the aim, the greater its power to shape you.

When your desire aligns with your inner values, it becomes more than a wish—it becomes a calling. That is enough. But you may also want to choose a goal that benefits others, adding depth and dimension to your path. In doing so, your desire becomes a force for harmony.

The most powerful desires are not isolated; they ripple outward. They uplift not only your life, but the lives you touch.

Next, use your imagination to embody the experience of already having what you desire. Write it down, read it, speak it aloud, visualize it vividly, and deeply feel its presence—not as something to chase, but as something already alive within you.

Whether your goal is external and material, it always reflects something within. You are not just building toward something— you are building into yourself. A meaningful desire, when chosen with intention, becomes a symbol of your inner truth—revealed step by step through action.

A thought held with emotion becomes a vibration—subtle, resonant, and alive. When you return to the practice of envisioning your desire, feeling it as real, and acting in alignment with it, you embed that intention into the subconscious. Your Higher Self responds by aligning thought and feeling, perception and behavior. Slowly, your attention filters toward what supports your vision. Circumstances begin to shift. Patterns emerge. Life reflects your internal structure.

This is how the invisible becomes visible—not through force, but through frequency—through the resonance of aligned thought, feeling, and action. In this alignment, flow arises—not as effort, but as resonance. This is where the work of building yourself becomes indistinguishable from creating your experience in the world.

Flow is the state in which your thoughts, emotions, and actions move in harmony toward a meaningful aim. It is not the absence of challenge, but the absence of inner resistance. In flow, effort feels natural and life may begin to respond through synchronicities—those meaningful coincidences that reflect alignment between your inner world and outer reality.

Still, belief fluctuates. And inner harmony is not a constant state. Both must be cultivated. When you find yourself slipping into doubt or losing momentum, return to presence. Take inventory of your current emotional and energetic state without judgment. Use breath, stillness, or movement to reconnect with your body. Speak your intention aloud. Journaling your original "why"—the reason behind your vision—can reignite inner trust.

You may want to create daily rituals that anchor belief through repetition—visual cues, affirmations, or brief moments of reflection. These are not magical acts; they are reminders. Belief is strengthened not by thought alone, but by each action that reflects your trust. Each time you take aligned action, even in uncertainty, you reinforce your own trustworthiness. That is how flow returns—not through control, but through consistent willingness. The Higher Self responds most clearly when you act with quiet confidence, not loud certainty.

And in this space, you realize what you've been seeking was never elsewhere—it has always lived within you. Clarity. Purpose. Connection. Not to be found, but remembered.

Integration isn't a destination but a state of being, deepening naturally over time. You stop second-guessing your choices and begin living from confident presence.

To sustain this alignment, elemental balance is essential. **Water** and **Earth** anchor your emotions in stable, grounded action, while **Fire** and **Air** unite your passion with clear insight. Together, they embody the ancient principle "As above, so below," harmonizing your spiritual and physical worlds. From the equilibrium of this balanced center emerges Gnosis, the still, intuitive awareness guiding your actions.

Integration requires daily nourishment. Engage regularly in meditation to nurture inner clarity, exercise for physical vitality, sunlight to energize and align your natural rhythms, restorative time in nature to reconnect with life's inherent beauty, and reflective reading and journaling to inspire continual growth.

These simple, powerful practices reinforce your equilibrium and help you fully embody your wisdom.

Balance doesn't require perfection. Some days may feel structured and energized, others may feel scattered or still. Equilibrium is found not in control, but in responsiveness, by noticing your needs and adjusting with care. Whether your practice is quiet or expressive, brief or extended, it is enough.

The Master Key is more than a concept. It is a way of being. You are both builder and temple, seeker and source, mirror and light. The pyramid is no longer external; it symbolizes your ongoing transformation.

Pause now to assess your inner elemental balance: Earth (stability), Water (emotion), Air (thought), Fire (action), and Spirit (connection). Identify which feels most aligned and which needs gentle adjustment. Choose one achievable step this week to reinforce your harmony and alignment. As you act from this clarity, life will begin responding in ways that reflect the depth of your alignment—subtly, steadily, and often beyond your expectations.

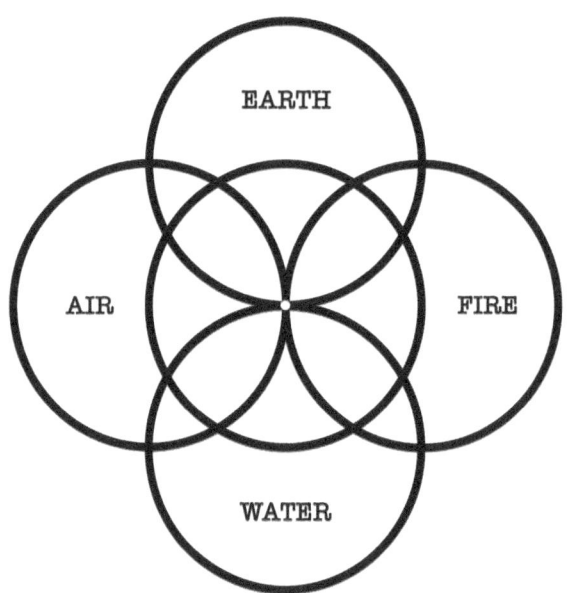

Chapter 13: Overcoming Challenges
The Path of Mastery

The path of spiritual mastery is beautiful, but it is not without difficulty. Every transformation stirs resistance. Every new level of awareness invites deeper responsibility.

To walk this path fully, you must learn to meet challenges not as obstacles, but as invitations. What looks like setback is often initiation.

The most common challenges don't arrive as dramatic events. They show up as states: anxiety, depression, and aimlessness. These aren't signs of failure, but signals—pointing to parts of you that need care, attention, and alignment. If these states feel overwhelming or prolonged, seeking professional support is not weakness—it's wisdom. This path was never meant to be walked alone. The practices in this book are not a replacement for clinical care, but they can serve as spiritual companions—tools for reflection, reconnection, and self-direction.

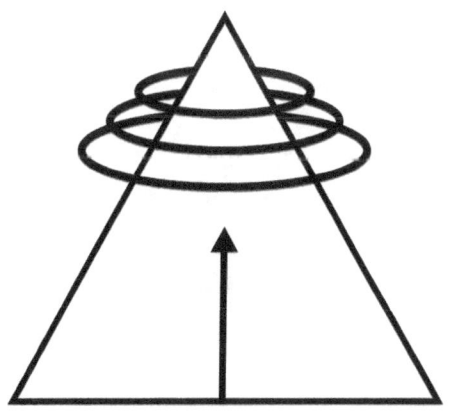

Centered and Balanced

Anxiety often arises when the future feels uncertain or too vast. The mind races; the body tightens; and the unknown becomes overwhelming. Beneath it all, anxiety is rooted in fear: fear of making the wrong choice, fear of failure, fear of letting go of control. Energetically, anxiety often reflects an excess of Air—too much thinking—without enough Earth to ground, or Water to settle.

The remedy is simplicity. Choose one small next step. Return to what you know. Practice meditation to move away from your thoughts and into your body through the heart and gut. Listen to your inner clarity, even if it whispers. Each small decision grounds you. Each act of courage builds momentum.

Ask yourself: What is this fear trying to teach me? What can I learn from this feeling? How can I practice trusting myself more deeply?

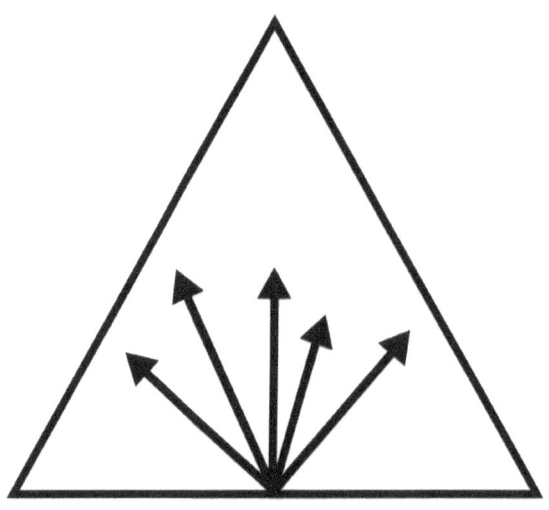

Fear & Anxiety

Depression, while complex, often emerges when your inner elements are out of balance. Too much thinking without emotional expression. Too much effort without grounding. Too much isolation without connection. A weakened Fire can dull your sense of purpose, while a neglected Spirit can leave you feeling disconnected from meaning.

The shift begins with presence. Come back to your body. Rest. Breathe. Move gently. Express what you're feeling, without shame or analysis. And then, when you're ready, begin again. One breath. One act. One step. Simple practices such as journaling, meaningful conversations, and regularly expressing gratitude for what is good—no matter how small—can offer gentle yet powerful relief, gradually guiding you back to equilibrium.

You don't need to fix everything all at once. The past does not define your future; it prepares you for it. Start by connecting to how you feel right now. Notice and accept your current emotions without trying to change or judge them. Then, gently take one step forward.

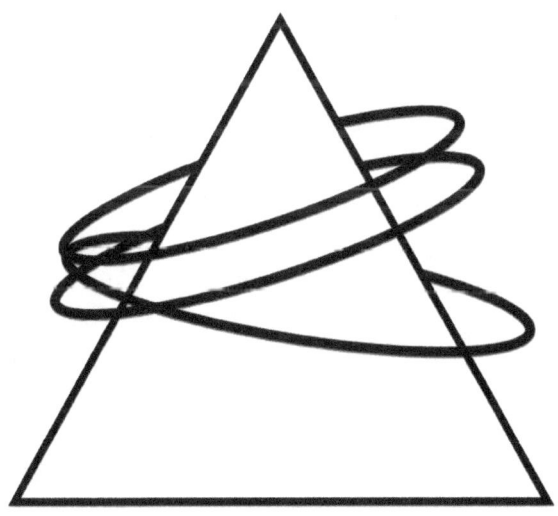

Depression

Aimlessness is the most subtle challenge. While disorienting at first, over time it can become destructive. When you lack direction, your energy diffuses. Days drift. This often reflects a disconnection from Spirit—or a scattered Air element with no grounding from Earth.

If you don't choose a path for yourself, someone or something else eventually will. And in following a direction that doesn't align with your own, you may lose touch with your Higher Self and your journey of becoming.

Self-direction is the first act toward freedom. Start with reflection. What matters to me now? What do I love, fear, or long for? What vision would I follow, even without a guarantee?

Then, choose a simple, meaningful direction. An aim to work toward. It might relate to a relationship, a project, a new skill, a place to go, or something your heart has carried for years. With the goal in mind, clarify a first step.

Even an imperfect aim is better than none. Direction gives shape to your days. Purpose creates momentum. And if you're feeling overwhelmed or unsure where to begin, know this: even choosing to pause, breathe, and observe your thoughts is an act of direction. Small shifts in awareness are how the path begins to open.

Happiness is not the goal; it's the byproduct of purposeful engagement. You don't chase it—you create it by stepping outside your comfort zone, living with integrity, and acting with courage and intention.

So pause and ask yourself: Where am I still stuck in fear, doubt, or confusion? What small act of clarity or inner alignment could I take today? What would it mean to begin again, now, with love?

That small act becomes the next stone in your pyramid. That step, however imperfect, points you toward the light of truth.

In action, your Higher Self will emerge to guide you. Have no fear and follow its lead.

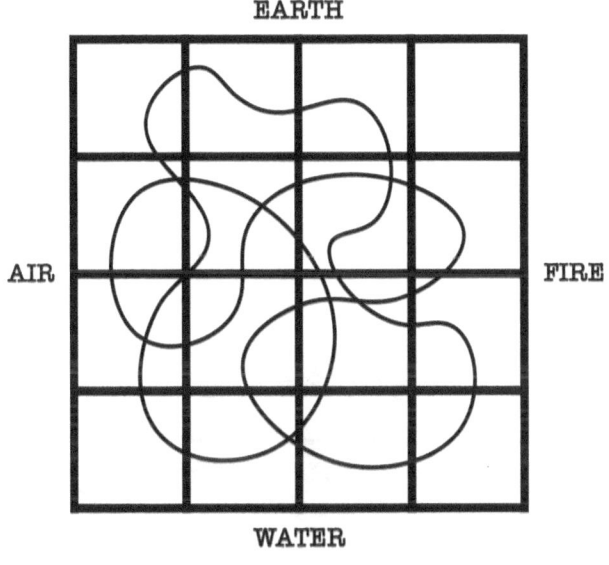

Aimlessness

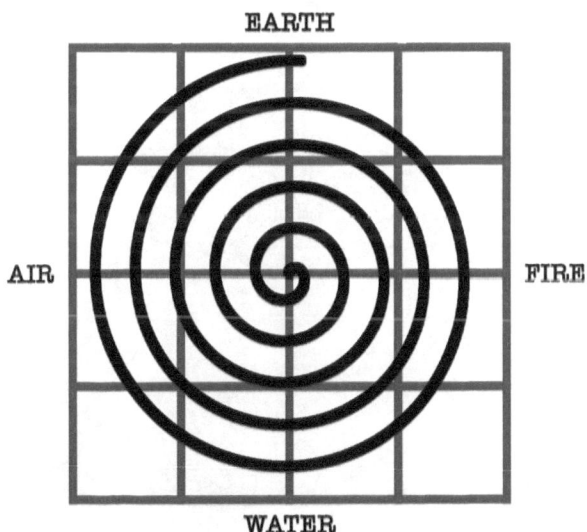

Centered and Balanced

Chapter 14: In Closing

A Reprise for Reflection

As you arrive at the end of this journey, something deeper has likely stirred within you. You've walked through a complete framework of conscious creation and self-discovery—guided by ancient symbols, natural rhythms, and your own inner knowing. What once seemed hidden has now become familiar. The mystery has unfolded, not as something outside of you, but as something long waiting to be remembered.

The truths encoded in the Great Seal and the pyramid are no longer abstract. You now clearly see yourself as the conscious creator of your reality. The power to shape your life has never existed in some future version of you. It has always been within, waiting patiently for your recognition, your trust, and your full participation in the unfolding of your path.

Through the threefold journey, you've reclaimed this truth. Self-Realization awakened you to your authentic nature. Divine Manifestation invited you to actively live from that truth. The Master Key revealed the alignment and clarity required to consciously co-create your reality.

This truth is not something you only find; it is something you embody.

The pyramid remains your map. Each choice is a stone. Each moment, an offering. Each step, a spiral upward.

Even if your vision is not yet fully realized, trust that the process is already underway. It asks not for perfection, only your presence.

The journey of conscious creation isn't about controlling outcomes. It's about co-creating with trust. When your inner world aligns, the outer world responds. When you move with clarity, life meets you halfway—often in surprising and beautiful ways.

True freedom begins with self-direction. When you choose your path with intention, your power returns to you. When you honor your truth, the universe listens.

As you consciously shape your reality, remember that your journey is woven into the greater tapestry of humanity. Approach others with compassion, knowing that every individual you encounter is quietly constructing their own inner pyramid, often unseen. Recognize your responsibility both to yourself and to the world around you.

Your path may not look like anyone else's. It may move slowly, unfold in cycles, or pause for breath. That does not make it less true. Trust your rhythm. Trust your way of knowing.

And always remember that you are enough, just as you are.

And you have so much to be grateful for.

Every life experience, even the imperfect, uncertain, and unpolished, is part of your sacred unfolding.

You are not off track; you are in motion.

Take a moment now. Breathe. Feel both the weight and the lightness of all you've discovered.

And when you're ready, step forward. Whether with boldness or stillness, certainty or curiosity, move toward the vision that speaks to your soul. Because now you know:

You are the beginning and the end.

The architect and the creation.

You are that you are.

You are the Higher Self,

made manifest through creative action.

The pyramid is no longer just a symbol. It is a mirror.

In it, you've seen your truest self.

Align with that self, and the universe will respond.

Reality bends to those who walk with clarity and purpose.

May you always be guided by truth, anchored in courage, and led by love.

Your truest and purest identity is ineffable.
Through the Pyramid of Self,
it begins to take shape.
You move closer with each stone,
each cycle, each phase,
each project or goal.

What you build will not be perfect.
It is not meant to be.
It is meant to be honest. Authentic.
And yours.

In your Pyramid of Self,
the capstone is the stone to be found.
It is detached from its base,
just as it appears on the one-dollar bill.
The seeker is the builder.

To know thyself
is the pursuit of becoming whole.

Endnotes

The following notes reference the canonical text provided in the preface. You will find that the quotes and excerpts are drawn from diverse sacred traditions and philosophical teachings. Where possible, direct quotations from public-domain translations have been provided. In some cases, passages are given in paraphrased form; these are clearly noted and drawn from public teachings or oral traditions where no direct citation is available.

These sources are offered to highlight the timeless and universal nature of humanity's quest for truth. Each tradition referenced offers a unique perspective, yet together they affirm a universal wisdom: the realization that we are inherently connected to something greater. Recognizing this connection aligns us with the creative forces of the universe, awakening a deeper purpose and understanding within our lives.

Line 1:
"Within you is the Master Key to all creation."

Corpus Hermeticum (Hermetic tradition)
"This Mind in men is God…"
— Corpus Hermeticum XII (XIII), "About the Common Mind," trans. G. R. S. Mead, 1906

Gospel of Thomas (Gnostic Christianity)
"If you bring forth what is within you, what you have will save you; if you do not have it within you, what you do not have within you [will] kill you."
— Saying 70, trans. Mark M. Mattison

Īśā Upaniṣad (Vedic tradition)
"And he who beholds all beings in the Self, and the Self in all beings, he never turns away from it."
— v. 6, trans. Max Müller, Sacred Books of the East 1 (1879)

Bhagavad Gītā (Hindu tradition)
"I am the self, O Guḍākeśa! seated in the hearts of all beings; I am the beginning and the middle and the end also of all beings."
— 10.20, trans. K. T. Telang, Sacred Books of the East 8 (1882)

Mahāparinirvāṇa Sūtra (Mahāyāna Buddhism)
"一切眾生悉有佛性" — "All beings have Buddha-nature."
— Taishō Tripiṭaka T12, no. 374 (Chinese canon, 1924 edition)

Òdu Ifá (Yorùbá tradition; proverb)
"Orí inú ni olúwa orí." ("The inner head is the master of the outer head.")
— Traditional Yorùbá teaching (oral transmission; paraphrase)

Line 2:
"What is above is reflected below, what is within is mirrored without. May the one great work be completed."

Emerald Tablet (Hermetic tradition)
"That which is below is like that which is above; and that which is above is like that which is below."
— Isaac Newton's English translation (c. 1680; printed 1893)

Confessio Fraternitatis (Rosicrucian tradition, 1615)
"Although that great Book of Nature stand open to all Men, yet there are but few that can read and understand the same."
— *Confessio Fraternitatis*, Eng. trans. Thomas Vaughan (1652)

Gospel of John (Christian tradition)
"At that day ye shall know that I am in my Father, and ye in me, and I in you."
— John 14:20, King James Version (1611)

Chāndogya Upaniṣad (Vedic tradition)
"That which is the subtle essence, in it all that exists has its self. It is the True. It is the Self. And thou, O Śvetaketu, art it."
— 6.8.7, trans. Max Müller, *Sacred Books of the East* 1 (1879)

Sefer Yetzirah (Kabbalistic tradition)
"Their end is even as their beginning, joined to the One, even as a flame is bound to the coal."
— 1:7, trans. W. W. Westcott (1887)

Line 3:
"The journey begins in unity.
Spirit descending into form.
The spiritual self on high to the material self below."

Plotinus (Neoplatonic philosophy)
"The Soul, then, of the All—life, abundant through all the universe—descended from the Intellectual-Principle for the purpose of care for what was to come."
— *Enneads* IV.8.5, trans. Stephen MacKenna (1917–1930)

Bhagavad Gītā (Hindu tradition)
"I am the origin of all; from Me all things proceed."
— 10.8, trans. K. T. Telang, *Sacred Books of the East* 8 (1882)

Guru Granth Sahib (Sikhism)
"The Word of the Guru's Shabad is the sound-current of the Naad; the Word of the Guru's Shabad is the wisdom of the Vedas; the Word of the Guru's Shabad is all-pervading."
— *Japji Sahib*, Paurī 5, Khalsa Consensus Translation (1993)

Kabbalah (Jewish mystical tradition)
The Zohar describes divine light as emanating through the sefirot, descending from higher worlds to lower.
— *Sefer ha-Zohar* (paraphrase)

Gospel of John (Christian tradition)
"And the Word was made flesh, and dwelt among us."
— John 1:14, King James Version (1611)

Kebra Nagast (Ethiopian Orthodox)
"And the Spirit of God dwelt in the flesh of Adam, the first man."
— *Kebra Nagast*, ch. 3, trans. E. A. Wallis Budge (1922)

Line 4:

"From this connection arises the divine spark.
The process of becoming whole. The fragmented
aspects of your being harmonize under the light of
divine awareness. Out of many, one."

Popol Vuh (Maya tradition)
"Yellow corn and white corn were the substance of the body of
man; their blood was of water, their flesh of corn."
— Popol Vuh, trans. Lewis Spence (1908)

Gāthās of Zarathustra (Zoroastrianism)
"He who makes his thought (good) is a promoter of the true
Dominion, and (thereby) a benefactor of Thy Spirit, O Mazda
Ahura."
— Yasna 31.22, trans. L. H. Mills, Sacred Books of the East 31
(1887)

Bṛhadāraṇyaka Upaniṣad (Vedic tradition)
"This self (ātman) is Brahman, the immortal, the fearless.
Verily, he who knows this becomes the Self indeed.
And thus it is declared: 'I am Brahman.'"
— 1.4.10, trans. Max Müller, Sacred Books of the East 15 (1884)

Ibn ʿArabī, Fuṣūṣ al-Ḥikam (Sufi mysticism)
The cosmos is the outward form of Reality; the human being is
its inward locus.
— Attributed to Ibn ʿArabī (paraphrase)

Lakota teaching (Indigenous North America)
All things are kindred; in sympathy they teach and heal.
— Traditional Lakota teaching (oral transmission; paraphrase)

Line 5:
"When you align the Lower Self
with the Higher Self,
the creator awakens."

Freemasonry
"The Temple which the Freemason is building is with him,
in his own heart."
— Albert G. Mackey, *An Encyclopedia of Freemasonry*, vol. 2 (1874)

Lakota — White Buffalo Calf Woman (Indigenous tradition)
When heart and mind are one, the power of the universe aids
the request.
— Oral teaching attributed to White Buffalo Calf Woman
(paraphrase)

Rosicrucian Order
"For the true philosophy, which is the knowledge of nature, is
imprinted in man, and only requires to be renewed and brought
again to light."
— *Confessio Fraternitatis*, Eng. trans. Thomas Vaughan (1652)

Analects (Confucianism)
"When we see men of a contrary character, we should turn
inwards and examine ourselves."
— 4.17, trans. James Legge, *The Chinese Classics*, vol. 1 (1893)

Line 6:
"The energy of creative chaos appears.
Waves of potentiality in a state of confusion."

Tao Te Ching (Taoist tradition)
"The Nameless was the beginning of Heaven and Earth; the Named was the mother of all things."
— Chapter 1, trans. James Legge, *Sacred Books of the East*, vol. 39 (1891)

Hesiod — Theogony (Greek tradition)
"First Chaos came to be, and next broad-bosomed Earth..."
— Lines 116–118, trans. H. G. Evelyn-White, *Hesiod: The Homeric Hymns and Homerica* (1914)

Kojiki (Shintō tradition)
"When chaos began to condense, before Heaven and Earth had separated, names were not yet given, nor deeds done."
— *Kojiki*, Section I.5, trans. Basil Hall Chamberlain (1882)

Memphite Theology (Ancient Egypt)
"It is Ptah, the very great, who gave life to all the gods and their kas through this heart and through this tongue. For every word of the god came about through what the heart devised and the tongue commanded. Thus were fashioned all things, and all the gods as well, and every divine word was brought into being."
— Shabaka Stone, trans. J. H. Breasted, *Development of Religion and Thought in Ancient Egypt* (1912), pp. 50–51

Dogon cosmology (West Africa)
The primordial point of potential and the creative Word (*Amma*).
— Traditional Dogon teaching (oral transmission; paraphrase)

Line 7:
"Through intention, balance, and action, chaos transmutes into harmony, purpose, and order."

Genesis (Biblical creation)
"And God said, Let there be light: and there was light."
— Genesis 1:3, King James Version (1611)

Sefer Yetzirah (Kabbalistic tradition)
"He formed Substance out of Chaos, and made Non-Existence into Existence."
— 2:6, trans. W. W. Westcott (1887)

Heraclitus (Greek philosophy)
"The harmony of the world is of opposites, as of the bow and the lyre."
— Fragment B51, trans. John Burnet, Early Greek Philosophy (1892)

Yìjīng — Great Treatise (Chinese philosophy)
"In the Changes there is the Great Primal Beginning; from it came the two elementary forms."
— Xì Cí Zhuàn (Great Treatise), trans. James Legge, Sacred Books of the East 16 (1899)

Farīd al-Dīn ʿAṭṭār, Conference of the Birds (Persian Sufism)
"Presence of the Source turns chaos into a dance of order."
— After Edward FitzGerald's epitome (1889) (paraphrase)

Line 8:
Manifest the Higher Self through creative action. Allow the essence of the divine to take tangible form in the material world."

Tao Te Ching (Taoist tradition)
"The Tao produced One; One produced Two; Two produced Three; and Three produced all things."
— Chapter 42, trans. James Legge, *Sacred Books of the East*, vol. 39 (1891)

Śiva Sūtras (Hindu tantra)
From awakened awareness, creation manifests through focused will.
— Traditional Kashmir Śaiva teaching (paraphrase)

Hekhalot Rabbati (early Jewish mysticism)
The heavenly vision is brought into deed, so that the divine word may be manifest among humankind.
— Early Hekhalot tradition (paraphrase)

Builders of the Adytum (Western esotericism)
Will and wisdom unite; mind conceives and hands create.
— Teaching attributed to Paul Foster Case (paraphrase)

Corpus Hermeticum (Hermetic tradition)
"For it is by the Word that all things are made, and the Mind is the Father of the Word."
— *Corpus Hermeticum* I (Poimandres), trans. G. R. S. Mead, *Thrice Greatest Hermes* (1906)

Line 9:
"The elements guide the way: Earth grounds and builds. Water cleanses and nurtures. Air brings clarity and insight. Fire ignites passion and transformation. Spirit unites."

Qur'ān (Islamic cosmology)
"We made every living thing of water."
— 21:30, trans. J. M. Rodwell, The Koran (1861)

Empedocles (Greek elemental philosophy)
"Hear first the four roots of all things: Zeus, Hera,
Aidoneus, and Nestis."
— Fragment B6 (via Simplicius), trans. John Burnet, *Early Greek Philosophy* (1892)

Suśruta Saṃhitā (Āyurveda)
"This animated organism is composed of the five fundamental material principles…"
— Sūtrasthāna ch. XLVI, trans. Kaviraj Kunjalal Bhishagratna (1911)

Modern Druidry (OBOD)
In the Sacred Grove: Land, Sea, and Sky; the four elements within the Circle; the Spirit (Awen) that unites.
— Contemporary OBOD teaching
(oral transmission; paraphrase)

Māori (Aotearoa New Zealand)
"Ko au te awa, ko te awa ko au."
("I am the river, and the river is me.")
— Traditional Whanganui iwi proverb (oral transmission)

Line 10:
"In equilibrium lies mastery."

Hermetic maxim (Western esotericism)
"Equilibrium is the basis of the Great Work."
— Golden Dawn maxim (modern source; paraphrase)

Tao Te Ching (Taoist inner cultivation)
"He who stands on tiptoe does not stand firm; he who stretches his legs does not walk easily."
— Chapter 24, trans. James Legge,
Sacred Books of the East 39 (1891)

Pirkei Avot (Judaism)
"Which is the right path for a man to choose? That which is praiseworthy to him who pursues it, and praiseworthy in the sight of men."
— Avot 2:1, trans. Charles Taylor, *Sayings of the Fathers* (1897)

Rosicrucian Order
Balance of body, mind, and spirit is taught as the condition for mastery.
— Oral teaching (paraphrase)

Bhagavad Gītā (Hindu scripture)
"Be steadfast in yoga, O Arjuna. Perform your duty, abandoning attachment, and remaining balanced in success and failure. Equilibrium is called yoga."
— 2.48, trans. K. T. Telang, *Sacred Books of the East* 8 (1882)

Line 11:
"The pyramid is your map, a framework of creation.
Its base provides stability,
its apex shines with the All-Seeing Eye
—divine awareness connecting you to eternal Source."

Egyptian Pyramid Texts (Old Kingdom)
"Opened are the double doors of the horizon; unlocked are
its bolts."
— *Pyramid Texts*, Utterance 302, cited in J. H. Breasted,
Development of Religion and Thought in Ancient Egypt (1912)

Freemasonry — All-Seeing Eye
"The All-Seeing Eye ... may be considered a symbol of God
manifested in His omnipresence... It is a symbol of the
Omnipresent Deity."
— Albert G. Mackey, *An Encyclopedia of Freemasonry*, vol. 1 (1873)

Fama Fraternitatis (Rosicrucian tradition)
"We have a House, which we call the House of the Holy Spirit."
— Early English editions (17th c.)

Aboriginal Songlines (Australian Indigenous)
Country is a living map of ancestral journeys; sacred sites are
verses in an ongoing song.
— Traditional Aboriginal teaching
(oral transmission; paraphrase)

Line 12:
"Take responsibility for your path.
Become both the builder and the temple."

Bhagavad Gītā (Hindu scripture)
"Let a man raise himself by himself; let him not lower himself...
for self is the friend of self."
— 6.5, trans. K. T. Telang, *Sacred Books of the East* 8 (1882)

Orphic Hymn to Zeus (Orphic mysteries)
"Jove is the first and last, high thund'ring king; middle
and head; from Jove all beings spring."
— Hymn 15, trans. Thomas Taylor, *The Mystical Hymns
of Orpheus* (1792)

Guru Granth Sahib (Sikhism)
"As you plant, so shall you harvest."
— *Sri Guru Granth Sahib*, Ang 134, trans. Sant Singh Khalsa
(1993, released public domain)

1 Corinthians (Christianity)
"Know ye not that ye are the temple of God, and that the Spirit
of God dwelleth in you?"
— 3:16, King James Version (1611)

Hausa (West African wisdom)
"He who has no patience cannot build a house."
— Hausa proverb, collected in George G. Kraft,
Hausa Proverbs (1915)

Julian of Norwich (Christian mysticism)
"All shall be well, and all shall be well, and all manner of thing
shall be well."
— *Revelations of Divine Love*, trans. Grace Warrack (1901)

Line 13:
"With time, each choice becomes another stone upon your foundation. Life spirals upward in wisdom, each experience marking your ascent."

Sefer Yetzirah (Kabbalistic tradition)
"He engraved them, hewed them, combined them, weighed them; and with them He formed all that was formed and all that would be formed."
— 2:2, trans. W. W. Westcott (1887)

Lotus Sūtra (Mahāyāna Buddhism)
"By means of one sole vehicle, the Buddha-vehicle, do I teach creatures the Law; there is no second vehicle, nor a third."
— Chapter 2, trans. Hendrik Kern, *Sacred Books of the East*, vol. 21 (1884)

H. P. Blavatsky (Theosophy)
"Karma is the unerring law which adjusts effect to cause, on the physical, mental and spiritual planes of being."
— *The Key to Theosophy* (1889)

Kumulipo (Hawaiian creation chant)
"At the time that turned the heat of the earth, / At the time when the heavens turned and were set apart…"
— Opening lines, trans. Martha Warren Beckwith, *The Kumulipo* (1906)

Andean teachings (Q'ero)
Ayni—reciprocity with all life—interweaves destiny with all relations.
— Traditional Q'ero teaching (oral transmission; paraphrase)

Line 14:
"Intuition is the voice of your Higher Self. Trust its guidance even when the path seems uncertain. The journey itself is the reward."

Hávamál (Norse wisdom literature)
"The wary guest who to the feast comes keeps silent with listening ear; his ears open, his eyes observant: so he explores all around."
— Stanza 7, trans. Benjamin Thorpe, *Edda Sæmundar Hinns Fróða* (1866)

Bhagavad Gītā (Hindu scripture)
"But the man who is full of faith, devoted to it, and who has subdued the senses, obtains knowledge; having obtained knowledge, he quickly attains tranquillity."
— 4:39, trans. K. T. Telang, *Sacred Books of the East*, vol 8 (1882)

Rūmī (Sufi mysticism)
"Love is the astrolabe of God's mysteries."
— *Masnavī-i Ma'navī*, Book I, trans. R. A. Nicholson (1926)

Aboriginal Dreaming (Australia)
The land teaches; listening reveals oneself.
— Aboriginal teaching (oral transmission; paraphrase)

Layman P'ang (Chan/Zen)
"My supernatural power and marvelous activity: drawing water and carrying firewood."
— Attributed to Layman P'ang (8th c. Chan master)

Line 15:
"Aimlessness is fear made manifest. If you do not direct your journey, another will. It is better to choose, to err, and refine than remain lost in indecision."

Plato — Apology (Greek philosophy)
"The unexamined life is not worth living."
— 38a, trans. Benjamin Jowett, *The Dialogues of Plato* (1892 rev.)

Bhagavad Gītā (Hindu scripture)
"Better is one's own duty, though wanting, than the duty of another well discharged."
— 3:35, trans. K. T. Telang, *Sacred Books of the East*, vol. 8 (1882)

Marcus Aurelius — Meditations (Stoic philosophy)
"In the morning when thou risest unwillingly, let this thought be present— I am rising to the work of a human being."
— 5.1, trans. George Long, *The Meditations of Marcus Aurelius Antoninus* (1862)

Dante Alighieri — Inferno (Medieval Christian literature)
"Midway upon the journey of our life I found myself within a forest dark, for the straightforward pathway had been lost."
— Canto I, lines 1–3, trans. H. W. Longfellow,
The Divine Comedy (1867)

Yorùbá proverb (West African wisdom)
"However far the stream flows, it never forgets its source."
— Traditional Yorùbá proverb (oral transmission)

Line 16:
"When your pyramid nears completion, it reveals not an ending, but the eternal truth: you are both beginning and end, seeker and destination."

Corpus Hermeticum (Hermetic tradition)
In the One, beginning and end are joined.
— Corpus Hermeticum, trans. G. R. S. Mead, Thrice Greatest Hermes (1906)

Bardo Thödol — The Tibetan Book of the Dead (Vajrayāna Buddhism)
"O nobly-born... thy present intellect, in real nature, void, not formed into anything as regards characteristics or colour, is the real state of the Void."
— trans. W. Y. Evans-Wentz, The Tibetan Book of the Dead (1927)

Book of Revelation (Christianity)
"I am Alpha and Omega, the beginning and the end, the first and the last."
— Revelation 22:13, King James Version (1611)

Chrysopoeia of Cleopatra (alchemical emblem)
"Ἑν τὸ πᾶν." ("The All is One.")
— Ouroboros motto (Alexandrian manuscript, 3rd–4th c.)

Longchenpa (Vajrayāna)
Saṃsāra and nirvāṇa are known as one at the moment of recognition.
— Teaching attributed to Longchen Rabjam (oral transmission; paraphrase)

Line 17:
"You are the creator and the creation.
This is the new order for the ages."

Sufi teaching (often cited as ḥadīth qudsī)
"I was a hidden treasure and loved to be known, so I created creation that I might be known."
— Widely cited in Sufi literature; not in canonical ḥadīth (paraphrase)

Asclepius (Hermetic tradition)
"A great miracle, Asclepius, is man."
— Asclepius, in G. R. S. Mead, Thrice Greatest Hermes (1906)

Celtic Druid wisdom (Celtic tradition)
With each turning of the wheel, the wise both learn and teach.
— Traditional Druidic teaching (oral transmission; paraphrase)

Santo Daime (ayahuasca tradition)
"Eu sou filho da terra e do céu." ("I am child of earth and sky.")
— Traditional hymn (oral transmission; paraphrase)

Orphic Hymn to Protogonos (Orphic mysteries)
"From thee are all things, and in thee they all end, for thou art the Creator and thou the Destroyer."
— Hymn 6, trans. Thomas Taylor, *The Mystical Hymns of Orpheus* (1792)

Roman Tradition
"Now the last age of the Cumaean song has come; the great order of the ages is born anew."
— Virgil, *Eclogue IV* (c. 40 BCE), trans. H. R. Fairclough, *Loeb Classical Library* (1916)

Line 18:
"Align with your true self, and the universe unfolds its mysteries in your favor. In alignment, all is revealed."

Bhagavad Gītā (Hindu scripture)
"When his mind is set on Yoga... he sees the Self by the self and is satisfied in the Self."
— 6.20–21 (sel.), trans. K. T. Telang, *Sacred Books of the East*, vol. 8 (1882)

Tao Te Ching (Taoist philosophy)
"There was something undefined and complete, coming into existence before Heaven and Earth."
— Chapter 25, trans. James Legge, *Sacred Books of the East*, vol. 39 (1891)

Sefer Yetzirah (Kabbalistic tradition)
"In thirty-two paths of Wisdom did Yah... engrave His Name."
— 1:1, trans. W. W. Westcott (1887)

Diamond Sūtra (Mahāyāna Buddhism)
"A Bodhisattva should produce a mind which does not rely upon sights, sounds, smells, tastes, touchables, or objects of mind. He should produce a mind that does not rely on anything."
— *Diamond Sūtra*, ch. 14, trans. William Gemmell (1912)

Homeric Hymn to Demeter (Eleusinian mysteries)
"Happy is he among men who has seen these mysteries."
— Lines 480–482, trans. H. G. Evelyn-White, *Homeric Hymns* (1914)

Glossary of Key Terms

Aimlessness
A state of disconnection from personal direction or purpose. In the context of this book, it represents spiritual stagnation or a lack of self-guided intention, often leading to confusion or dissatisfaction.

Alignment
A state of harmony between your Lower Self and Higher Self, where thoughts, feelings, and actions are integrated and purposeful. Alignment leads to clarity, flow, and meaningful creation.

All-Seeing Eye
A symbol found at the top of the pyramid on the Great Seal of the United States. It represents divine awareness, inner vision, and the presence of a higher intelligence guiding human evolution.

Circumambulation
A ritual or symbolic walking in a circle, often used to reflect spiritual progress or initiation. In this book, it refers to movement around the pyramid in a spiral, either inward (self-realization) or outward (manifestation).

Divine Manifestation
The second step in the journey of the Pyramid of Self, where inner truth is expressed through outward, aligned action. It is the process of allowing Spirit to take form in the material world.

Elemental Balance
A state of internal harmony achieved through the conscious integration of the five elements: Earth (stability), Water (emotion), Air (clarity), Fire (action), and Spirit (connection). Each element represents a facet of human experience and spiritual growth.

Equilibrium
A steady state of internal balance where the spiritual and material aspects of self are aligned. In this book, it is the key to mastery and is developed through ongoing awareness, discipline, and responsiveness to one's needs.

Flow
A state of inner alignment in which thoughts, emotions, and actions move harmoniously toward a meaningful aim. In this book, flow reflects the absence of inner resistance and often arises during spiritually aligned action.

Freemasonry
A fraternal spiritual and philosophical tradition that uses allegory, symbolism, and ritual to teach moral development and the inner construction of character.

Gnosis
From the Greek word for "knowledge," Gnosis in this book refers to deep inner knowing—not intellectual, but intuitive. It represents the space between the Higher and Lower Self where insight becomes lived wisdom.

Hermeticism
An ancient spiritual and philosophical tradition rooted in Egypt and attributed to Hermes Trismegistus, a synthesis of the Greek god Hermes and the Egyptian god Thoth. Hermeticism emphasizes the unity of all things and the correspondence between the macrocosm and microcosm. Its principles include "as above, so below".

Higher Self
The divine, intuitive, and creative aspect of you that exists beyond time, ego, or personality. It holds your deepest truth, guides your evolution, and communicates through intuition, vision, and resonance.

Integration
The outcome of the third and final step in the Pyramid of Self framework. It is the full embodiment of wisdom, where intuition and action become one. Integration is the lived realization unlocked through The Master Key.

Lower Self
The everyday self, governed by personality, habits, and survival instincts. While necessary for navigating the material world, it must be harmonized with the Higher Self to experience alignment and flow.

Master Key
In the context of this book, a symbolic term for the unified state of alignment between the Higher and Lower Self. The Master Key unlocks your ability to consciously shape reality through thought, feeling, and inspired action.

Mystery School
A historical or spiritual institution that teaches esoteric wisdom through initiation, symbolism, and inner transformation. These teachings are not given as dogma, but as experiential truths to be discovered.

Rose of Venus
A five-pointed star pattern formed by Venus over an eight-year cycle as it orbits the sun. It represents harmony, beauty, and the unfolding of inner transformation.

Rosicrucian Philosophy
A mystical tradition rooted in 17th-century Europe that teaches the transformation of the self through spiritual insight, alchemical symbolism, and divine love.

Sacred Geometry
Geometric patterns and proportions found throughout nature that are believed to reflect universal order and spiritual design. Examples include the Golden Ratio and the Rose of Venus.

Self-Realization
The first step in the Pyramid of Self. It involves awakening to your true nature, releasing illusion, and recognizing your connection to a higher purpose.

Spiral
A symbol of growth, evolution, and cyclical progress. In this book, the spiral reflects your personal journey through time, where each return to a familiar place comes with greater awareness.

Synchronicity

A meaningful coincidence that reflects the harmony between your internal state and outer experience. Synchronicities signal alignment and often emerge when you act from your Higher Self.

Theosophy

A modern esoteric tradition founded in the 19th century that blends Eastern philosophy with Western mysticism. It teaches the evolution of consciousness, universal brotherhood, and the spiritual laws that guide inner development.

Universal Consciousness

It is the source of both the individual self and the Higher Self— the foundational field in which all separateness dissolves, and all beings return to the same essential origin.